JESUS *IS* A DEMOCRAT

ESSAYS ON THE TEACHINGS OF JESUS AND THE DEMOCRATIC PARTY PLATFORM

Edward A. Bacon

Carol Day

George H. Lower

Lois A. Aroian

Melody Oliphant

Copyright © George H. Lower

All rights reserved.

ISBN: 9798390422434

Dedication

This book is dedicated to Nancy Lower, who served our nation as Medical Director in the Peace Corps in Mauritania (West Africa). Nancy was responsible for the health of fifty young adult volunteers while they served our country for two years in the desert.

Acknowledgments

Our thanks to Joanna Brown of Hadley, Massachusetts, who, as a book author, was helpful with suggestions of how to proceed toward producing and publishing a book; to Julia Day, PhD, our book editor, who gave extra care to make sure the manuscript was ready for submission to Amazon; and to Emily J. Lower for all her computer work and contact with Amazon.

TABLE OF CONTENTS

INTRODUCTION: JESUS *IS* A DEMOCRAT   1
   George H. Lower

CHAPTER ONE: *NOT* AS THE WORLD GIVES   7
   Edward A. Bacon

CHAPTER TWO: "WOMAN, WHY DO YOU INVOLVE ME?"   23
   Carol Day

CHAPTER THREE: JESUS AND THE DEMOCRATS CARE ABOUT YOUR HEALTH AND HEALING   33
   George H. Lower

CHAPTER FOUR: JESUS'S PREFERENCE FOR THE POOR AND THE DEMOCRATIC PARTY   41
   Lois A. Aroian

CHAPTER FIVE: IMMIGRATION: WELCOMING THE STRANGER   65
   Melody Oliphant

Introduction

Jesus *IS* a Democrat

Rev. George H. Lower

Is it possible that there is a definite link between what Jesus said and did and our politics today? Some would state not to mix politics and religion. I believe that Jesus's teachings are how we should live and love our neighbor. The actions of political parties can reveal how to love our neighbor as ourselves. We will present for your consideration five areas of the ministry of Jesus which seem to be included in the actions of the Democratic Party in the United States.

As we look at the strange title of our small book, we realize that "IS" in the title is an important theological statement. Jesus IS alive with us today in a spiritual way. We are people of the Trinity. Jesus is here today as the Holy Spirit. His Spirit allows us to discern how Jesus's teachings are carried out in the world today.

Our chapter writers share the thoughts and actions of Jesus as he ministers with people. Jesus cares about the immigrant—the stranger among us; he cares about the health and healing of persons; he cares about the peace that we seek for ourselves and others; he cares about women and their needs; and Jesus cares about the poor among us.

We will attempt to show how Jesus's thoughts and actions are best shown in what the Democratic Party affirms. The Democratic Party's platform includes some of the five areas that we have highlighted. If the "carpenter from Nazareth" appeared today, where would he want to care for thy neighbor? Many of us believe he would want to show love and caring within the Democratic Party in our nation today. What do you think?

We recommend that readers familiarize themselves with the Democratic Party's 2020 platform to gain the most from our book. Our chapter writers have addressed themes found in the "Preamble," "Achieving Universal, Affordable, Quality Health Care," "Restoring and Strengthening our Democracy," and "Creating a 21st Century Immigration System" sections of the Democratic platform. For more information on the Democratic Party's positions, visit the "Where We Stand" page of their website: https://democrats.org/where-we-stand/.

Edward A. Bacon was born in 1952 on Long Island, New York to a religious and church-going family. His mother was church organist, and his father taught Sunday school for many years. They both served as deacons.

Edward's education included graduating from Valley Stream Central High School in 1970, South Eastern Bible College, Lakeland, FL, in 1976 (BA), Ashland Theological Seminary, Ashland, OH, in 1980 (MDiv), and Andover Newton Theological School, Newton Centre, MA, in 2013 (DMin). In 1971, he came to faith in Jesus Christ and began studying for the Christian ministry; he was ordained as an American Baptist minister in 1980. He served pastorates in four Baptist churches (in Ohio, New York, Maine, and Massachusetts) before retiring in 2018.

Edward and his wife Ruth have one daughter. He also has a son from a previous marriage and twin grand-daughters. He is now retired on Islesboro, Maine, where Ruth grew up and he served as pastor of the Second Baptist Church for eighteen years. They are active members of the church, and both serve as deacons.

Chapter One

NOT AS THE WORLD GIVES

Rev. Dr. Edward A. Bacon

O Lord, calm the waves of this heart; calm its tempests. Calm thyself, O my soul, so that the divine can act in thee. Calm thyself, O my soul, so that God is able to repose in thee, so that his peace may cover thee. Yes, Father in heaven, often have we found that the world cannot give us peace, O but make us feel that thou art able to give peace; let us know the truth of thy promise: that the whole world may not be able to take away thy peace.[1]

This prayer, by Danish theologian and philosopher Søren Kierkegaard (1813-1855), also called "the father of existentialism," encapsulates thoughts of Jesus and the subject of peace. It was this lack of inner calm that brings many seeking and finding, through faith in Jesus, the peace they sought from the "Prince of Peace" (Isaiah 9:6).

Young men my age had one thing on their minds in 1970, registering for the draft. Though in its final years, the war in Vietnam was still going strong. It was my first semester of college, and I had several decisions to make; to enlist or wait to be drafted, to apply for a college deferment or seek status as a conscientious objector. The government made the decision for me with the draft lottery. My number was 298, and so, I continued in college and didn't think much more about military service or the need for dodging the draft. However, it continued to bother me that many of my generation were serving and dying. Years later, I served as a chaplain in the Army Reserve; many of the men I served with were veterans of this war, and I grew to appreciate their service.

Around the time I registered for the draft, another important decision came my way, to accept Jesus Christ as my Savior. The two decisions ran on parallel lines, my thoughts about conscientious objection and my thoughts about religious faith. A friend in college who was a conscientious objector put it to me quite frankly. He said I wasn't religious enough for my appeal to be granted. This encouraged me to take my religious faith more seriously, which led to my belief in Christ and eventually to my following a call to Christian ministry.

For me, how I viewed Jesus's teaching on military participation would be a key element in this decision. An expression made popular through the 1896 book *In His* Steps by Charles Sheldon was "What would Jesus do?"[2] Would Jesus fight in a war? I believe that Jesus believed in the sanctity of human life—all human life was sacred. Jesus would not condone violence in any form, except possibly when he became enraged in the temple (Mark 11:15-17). For example, at his arrest, one of his disciples cut off the ear of the servant of the high priest. Jesus declared to his disciples, "all who take the sword will perish by the sword" (Matthew 26:52).

It is difficult to believe that Jesus would own a weapon, especially for the purpose of taking a human life. He did, however, encourage his disciples to carry a few weapons (Luke 22:35-38), but that was for defensive rather than offensive purposes. And so, on the subject of the right to bear arms, it would be advisable for people of faith to ask themselves, "What would Jesus do?"

* * *

> Peace I leave with you; my peace I give to you. I do not give to you as the world gives. Do not let your hearts be troubled, and do not let them be afraid (John 14:27, NRSV).

As Jesus spoke with his disciples on the night of his Last Supper, he felt the need to prepare them for the difficult days to come. Within the next couple of days, one of them would betray him and another would deny knowing him. He would be arrested, tried, convicted, and crucified. All they could do was watch and wonder what in the world was coming next? And so, thinking they would be next, they fled and hid. They were troubled; they were afraid. What could Jesus say to them that would help them in these crucial moments and prepare them for the days to come?

He spoke to them of peace, "my peace," "NOT...as the world gives." Our English word *peace* derives from the Latin word *pax*, which would have expressed itself in Jesus's time in the *pax Romana*, "Roman peace." This was the political peace that Rome gave, a peace established through conquest and brutality. It could be argued that maintaining this peace led to Jesus's crucifixion, as it was Pontius Pilate's responsibility to keep the peace by all means, which meant appeasing those who demanded Jesus's death saying, "Crucify him!"

Certainly, this wasn't the peace Jesus was leaving with his disciples. The Gospel of John was originally written in the Greek language. The word "peace" in the Greek language is *eirene*. However, Jesus did not say these words in Greek—he spoke Aramaic; his concept of peace would be much more in line with the Hebrew word *shalom*. Thus, Jesus did not say "*Pax* I leave with you" or "*Eirene* I leave with you," but rather "*Shalom* I leave with you; my *shalom* I give to you."

The word "shalom" is found throughout the Hebrew scriptures, the only "Bible" Jesus knew. He drew his inspired concept of peace from it and imparted this knowledge to his disciples. Therefore, Jesus's understanding of peace is found throughout the Bible in the Old Testament writings of those before him, in his own words passed on in the gospels, and in the New Testament writings of those who followed him.

The peace of Jesus is basically the same as the peace of God, which is pronounced in the words of the Aaronic blessing:

> The LORD bless you and keep you; the LORD make his face to shine upon you, and be gracious to you; the LORD lift up his countenance upon you, and give you PEACE (Numbers 6:24-26, NRSV).

* * *

To be given peace indicates that peace is a gift, not something we have earned through our own efforts, but a gift from God, an act of God's grace and mercy. However, certain conditions must exist for this gift to be received. In the same fourteenth chapter of John, Jesus said, "Do not let your hearts be troubled. Believe in God, believe also in me" (John 14:1). The first condition to receive the gift of peace is to have a receptivity for peace of mind, not letting our hearts be troubled. The second condition to receive this gift of peace is faith. The gift of divine peace can be received by those whose faith enables them to have a receptive, peaceful spirit.

It was Jesus's intention that the gift of peace would be available to all people. And so, he declared in his Sermon on the Mount, "Blessed are the peacemakers, for they will be called children of God" (Matthew 5:9). Often peacemakers, or individuals seeking peace, are thought to be pacifists. That would seem to be the case in what Jesus said in this sermon. Beginning with verse thirty-eight he said, "You have heard that it was said, 'An eye for an eye and a tooth for a tooth.' But I say to you, do not resist an evildoer. But if anyone strikes you on the right cheek, turn the other also" (Matthew 5:38). And, in verse forty-three he added, "You have heard that it was said, 'You shall love your neighbor and hate your enemy.' But I say to you, love your enemies and pray for those who persecute you, so that you may be children of your Father in heaven" ["children of God"] (Matthew 5:43).

Politics have been a cause for division in American society. Our states, rather than being united (i.e., The United States) are divided between the red (Republican), the blue (Democrat), and those in between. However, the followers of Jesus Christ (Christians) are scattered all over the political spectrum. Churches can become more divided over politics than theology. The causes for this are difficult to comprehend, but the divisions are clear. And so, what would Jesus do within the political spectrum?

In 1845, the meeting house of our church on Islesboro was built. Its building became such a source of contention in the community that a few years later, in 1853, another church was built. The meeting house of the original Baptist church, founded in 1791 was deemed unsuitable for continued use, as it was unheated. And so, a group from that church built a new meeting house in the southern part of the island. However, those who remained in the original meeting house decided to build their meeting house in the northern part of the island. It also became a controversy as to which of these new churches could claim the name "First Baptist Church." A council of mainland Baptist ministers decided the church built in 1845 would be called the "Second Baptist Church" and that built in 1853 would be called the "First Baptist Church." The peace of the church was disrupted over the issue of location.

In that same year of 1845, the Baptists of the southern states separated themselves from their northern brethren, thus forming the Southern Baptist Convention. The primary cause for this breach among Baptists was the subject of slavery. Northern Baptists did not want to support missionaries who were slave owners. And so, the Southern Baptists took their leave, forming their own denomination. Within twenty years the entire country, north and south, found itself in a Civil War, or "War Between the States," over this issue of slavery.

Several of my ancestors, who were staunch Baptists, fought in this war, for both the north and the south. One of my great-great-great-grandfathers was an elder of the Primitive Baptist Church in Tennessee. He was also a slave owner, and he and his wife spent the war in federal prisons for their "treasonous" preaching in support of the southern cause. To their dying day they believed that slavery was a divinely established institution. Two of their sons died in that war defending that belief. But how did their beliefs affect their politics?

* * *

> For he is our peace; in his flesh he has made both groups into one and has broken down the dividing wall, that is, the hostility between us (Ephesians 2:14, NRSV).

In the early Church there were two groups: Jewish converts (or "the circumcised") and Gentile converts. The Jewish converts were those who were of the Jewish faith prior to their coming to faith in Jesus Christ. They considered the Church to be an extension of their Jewish faith and did not cease to be Jewish once they believed Jesus to be the Messiah.

The Gentiles (meaning "Nations") were non-Jewish converts to Christianity. The first example of Gentiles converting to Christianity is found in Acts 10 when Peter had a vision informing him that "What God has made clean, you must not call profane." (Acts 10:15). While Peter considered the meaning of this vision, a message came from a Gentile in Caesarea named Cornelius asking Peter to come to his house. Following Peter's preaching, Cornelius and his entire family believed, received the gift of the Holy Spirit, and were baptized. Peter then reported this to the apostles in Jerusalem, who in time reached the decision,

"Then God has given even to the Gentiles the repentance that leads to life" (Acts 11:18).

However, this conflict within the early Church persisted, especially concerning the need to circumcise these Gentile converts, thus making them Jewish before they could become Christians. Paul addressed this issue in several of his epistles, such as that above from Ephesians, saying "[Jesus] is our peace." As a result, "he has made both groups into one" and "has broken down the dividing wall," which he defines as the source of "the hostility between us" (Ephesians 2:14). There is peace because Jesus is our peace. With all the differences between the Jewish and Gentile converts, Jesus was their common denominator, their common ground.

These conflicts with non-converted Jews continued until the Apostle Paul had enough. When Paul was in Corinth, "Every sabbath he would argue in the synagogue and would try to convince Jews and Greeks" (Acts 18:4). When the Jews opposed and reviled him, he proclaimed, "Your blood be on your own heads! I am innocent. From now on I will go to the Gentiles" (Acts 18:6).

* * *

> Those conflicts and disputes among you, where do they come from? Do they not come from your cravings that are at war within you? (James 4:1, NRSV).

There is no certainty that this was written by the same James who was mentioned at the Jerusalem council of Acts 15. Certain traditions speculate it was the same individual who was listed among the biological brothers of Jesus in Matthew 13:55. If he was the same individual, it would be interesting to consider how he had decided the conflict about Gentile converts while in this letter was dealing with similar conflicts and disputes. He said that the conflicts that manifest themselves around us are the result of the conflicts that exist within us. All individuals fight battles within themselves—conflicts between right and wrong, or, more probably, the conflict between the correct and the more correct. The history of Christianity is a history of conflict and how Christians chose to separate rather than find compromise around their common ground of faith in Jesus. The modern ecumenical movement is an attempt to alter this course, but will it succeed? Is Jesus our peace today? Is he our common denominator?

Christians today are just as divided as the national politics. As American citizens we try to maintain the safeguards of our Constitution, but the separation of church and state is by no means a settled argument. Matters that should be questions of faith and ethics have become political platforms. And matters that should be debated on the floor of Congress or the Supreme Court are preoccupying American pulpits.

In the preamble to the 2020 Democratic Party's platform it reads, regarding peace and international relations:

> Democrats will lead with diplomacy as our tool of first resort and mobilize our allies and partners to meet the tests none of us can meet on our own. We will stand up to the forces of authoritarianism, not aid or abet their rise, and we will speak and act with clarity and purpose on behalf of human rights wherever they are under threat.

If, as this book asserts, Jesus IS a Democrat, how would he stand on this platform? To address this question, this chapter has dealt with the subject of Jesus and peace. How did he understand peace, and what did he say and do to bring about peace in the world?

Democrats have not always been regarded as peacemakers. Consider, for example, that the United States' involvement in many of the wars of the last and current centuries were waged under Democratic administrations. Woodrow Wilson, a Democrat, was president when the United States entered the First World War. Franklin Roosevelt, a Democrat, was president when the United States entered the Second World War. Harry Truman, a Democrat, was president when the United States continued to fight in the Second World War and fought in Korea. John Kennedy and Lyndon Johnson, both Democrats, were president when the United States became involved in and escalated the war in Vietnam. The war in Afghanistan began under the Republican administration of George W. Bush but continued under the Democratic administration of Barack Obama and the Republican administration of Donald Trump and didn't end until the Democratic administration of Joseph Biden, making it the longest war in American history. Historically, which party is the party of peace?

Arguably, the United States' involvement in these wars was primarily for defensive rather than offensive purposes. As a great superpower in the world, the United States has certain obligations with other nations of the world. Membership in the United Nations and the North Atlantic Treaty Organization make it difficult for the United States to sit idly by while smaller countries are threatened, such as the 2022 crisis in Ukraine. It would seem almost impossible for us to remain isolated in this world in which we have so many international interests. Yet, at the same time, we don't want to be considered the world's police force. And, in this regard, the Democratic platform seems feasible and something that Jesus would perhaps even agree with in principle.

The possibility for God's peace in this world bent on self-destruction seems unlikely. The prayer of Kierkegaard, which opened this chapter sums it up. He wrote, "often have we found that the world cannot give us peace, O but make us feel that thou art able to give peace."[3] The peace of God, the peace Jesus gives, transcends all human concepts of peace, so much so that the Apostle Paul wrote that it "surpasses all understanding" and will even "guard your hearts and your minds in Christ Jesus" (Philippians 4:7).

It seems to this writer that the peace Jesus gives is the peace that starts from the bottom-up (or the top-down, depending on one's perspective). We begin by individually receiving peace in our hearts through a relationship of peace with God. This peace then enables the possibility of peaceful relationships with one another. These group relationships will then have a peaceful influence on the broader society. Segments of society can then come together to bring peace to the state, the nation, and even the world. Such peace becomes the responsibility of the individual, not the government, the assumption being that peaceful individuals can have a positive influence on world peace: "Let there be peace on earth, and let it begin with me."[4]

---

[1] Soren Kierkegaard, *The Prayers of Kierkegaard*, edited by P. F. Lefevre (The University of Chicago Press, 1956).
[2] Charles Sheldon, *In His Steps* (Federal Book Company, 1897).

[3] Soren Kierkegaard, *The Prayers of Kierkegaard*, edited by P. F. Lefevre (The University of Chicago Press, 1956).
[4] Jill Jackson-Miller and Sy Miller, "Let There Be Peace on Earth" (Hanson House, 1955).

Carol Day is a retired elementary school teacher. She is a mother of two daughters, a grandma, and host mother to five exchange students. Her home has been in Utah for close to forty years. She is an elder in the Presbyterian Church (USA). She is an active member of Presbyterian Women (PW) on local, state and synod levels. She has been a participant in the PW United States Mission Experience that explored issues of human trafficking, domestic violence, immigration, and homelessness. She participated in the Commission on the Status of Women (CSW) as a part of the Ecumenical Women at the United Nations and the PW United Nations. The theme of the CSW was on achieving gender equality and empowerment of all women and girls in the context of climate change as well as environment and disaster risk reduction policies and programs.

Chapter Two

"Woman, Why do You Involve Me?"[1]

Carol Day

Forty years ago, I recorded a Christmas folk music radio show on a cassette tape. It became my favorite yet was barely tolerated by my husband and children. Thus, my early probe into how Jesus relates to women began with a discordant "It wer'nt no picnic, it wer'nt no picture postcard. It was hard."[2] This John Pole anti-carol describes the birth of Jesus in harsh, realistic terms. This song was followed by the Dory Previn carol "Did Jesus have a baby sister? Was she bitter was she sweet? Did she practice in her mirror; Saviorette, Savior Women, Savior person, Save your breath."[3] In Laura Bates's 2016 book *Everyday Sexism*, women share their stories of sexism, street harassment, discrimination on the job, sexual assault, and rape. Bates tells us, "Women are silenced by both the invisibility and the acceptability of the problem."[4] In the New Testament Jesus acknowledges women, making them visible and heard by listening to their feelings. Jesus is fulfilling God's promise to be with us.

There are several interactions between Jesus and women, specifically in the New Testament. This chapter will lift up the stories of women by focusing on

Jesus's family and disciples and Jesus's miracles to look at them alongside the terms of the 2020 Democratic platform.

Family and Friends

Jesus's relationship with his mother Mary began in the womb. Mary visits Elizabeth, who was with child, and a silent husband, Zechariah (Luke 1:39-45). When Elizabeth's son John leapt, Elizabeth recognized that she was in the presence of the Messiah, and Mary burst into a hymn of praise. Jesus brought great joy and blessing to Mary and Elizabeth. The realities of an unwed pregnancy, a geriatric pregnancy, and the birth in a stable were struggles that these women bore. Jesus acknowledged them. They were lifted out of their humble lives to become main characters in a salvation story—visible, listened to, and blessed.

Baby Jesus fulfilled the prayers of the widow Anna. Anna was in the temple day and night worshiping, fasting, and praying. When she met Jesus, she was filled with God's love and hope for redemption (Luke 2:36-38).

As a twelve-year-old, Jesus stayed behind at the temple to the dismay of his mother. He had revealed his character to the scholars in the temple and reminded Mary of his Father's work he would be doing. Yet, he did return to Nazareth with Mary to grow in wisdom, stature, and favor with God and man (Luke 2:48-51).

As a young man, not quite ready to answer the call to his ministry, Jesus accompanies his mother to a wedding in Cana (John 2:1-11). His mother requests Jesus to replenish the beverage supply. In a "Mommm-not-yet reproach," he addresses his mother as "Woman," stating that his time had not come. Yet, he turns the water into wine, revealing a first glimpse of Glory. Mary is acknowledged, listened to.

In John 13:34-35, Jesus defines a disciple, "A new command I give you: love one another. As I have loved you, so you must love one another. By this everyone will know that you are my disciples, if you love one another." As Jesus drops in on his disciples Martha and Mary, Mary drops everything and sits rapt at Jesus feet (Luke 10:38-42). Martha is bustling around to prepare a meal for her beloved guest. Jesus acknowledges Mary's feelings that led to her choice and listens to Martha.

The Democratic platform states, "We will give hate no safe harbor."[5] In doing this Democrats demonstrate obedience to the new commandment to love one another. Like Mary in Luke 10: 38-42, the platform drops the rhetoric and conflict to act in love saying, "we will speak and act with clarity and purpose to pursue truth and promote racial healing." The Democratic vision is attuned to the Christian kindness: feeding the hungry and quenching people's thirst, welcoming the stranger and clothing the naked, caring for the sick and visiting the imprisoned. It is a communal commitment to meeting every human's basic needs envisioned in the PC(USA) Matthew 25 Initiative.

The Bible mentions Joanna, Susanna, and Mary Magdalene among Jesus's disciples. These women supported Jesus's ministry by their own means (Luke 8:1-3). In the Democratic platform we find "advancing gender equality enhances stability and economic prosperity around the world." Women disciples, women's equality, means support and stability that moves us closer to the model of unconditional love. Mary Magdalene, from whom Jesus drove seven demons, is the first to receive the form of the risen Christ (Mark 16:9). The care and support by the women disciples, even after the tragedy at the cross, led them to be present at the tomb to witness the glory of the resurrection.

Miracles

In another encounter, Jesus interacts with a woman who was not his mother but a foreigner, a Samaritan (John 4:7-29, 34). This comes about later in the day when the woman feels safe to come to the well and the disciples are gathering some food. This time Jesus requests a drink of water. He uses this request to draw out the woman to make her visible and allow her voice to be heard. He knows the choices she has made. He does this not to condemn her but to reveal to her the opportunity for salvation. He offers her living water to show her that the time has now come when the true worshipers will worship the Father in the Spirit and in truth, for they are the kind of worshipers the Father seeks. Laurie Levin's book *Call Me A Woman* gives a present-day explanation of Jesus's approach in this instance, "Holding each person in the space of infinite possibilities, not to something ascribed to them at birth, we become the people who can solve our greatest challenges, from personal squabbles at home, at school, and work, through government, nation by nation."[6] This leads me to see this quote from the Democratic platform Preamble, "diversity is our greatest strength. That protest is among the highest forms of patriotism. That our fates and fortunes are bound to rise and fall together. That even when we fall short of our highest ideals, we never stop trying to build a more perfect union." I see Jesus's conversation with a foreigner and a woman as honoring diversity, protesting gender norms, and offering the way to rise from her past actions to work towards a more perfect union.

The Pharisees tried to trick Jesus using a woman caught in adultery (John 8:1-11). They asked him to weigh in on the necessity of stoning her to death. Jesus used some nonverbal action to teach that day. He bent down and drew aimlessly in the sand. The questions kept coming until Jesus straightened up saying, "Let any one of you who is without sin be the first to throw a stone at her." The sinners left one by one. Jesus saw this woman, acknowledged her choices and feelings, and forgave her. The Democratic platform acknowledges the sins of racism, colonization, climate, economy, sexism, misogyny, anti-Semitism, anti-Muslim bigotry, and white supremacy. Democrats will protect and promote the equal rights of all our citizens—women, LGBTQ+ people, religious minorities, people with disabilities, Native Americans, and all who have experienced discrimination.

Jesus's ministry included healing and raising up women and girls, whether it was from twelve years of bleeding or acknowledging the life that still resided in the daughter of the synagogue leader in Matthew 9:18-26. This same respect is carried out by Peter in Acts 9:36-42 where Tabitha also known as Dorcas responds to Peter's prayer at her deathbed, requesting to get up by opening her eyes, sitting up, and taking Peter's hand to stand. Tabitha's role as a disciple in the port city of Joppa was to provide clothing and care for the poor and widows. Tabitha's death and life story led many to believe in Jesus throughout Joppa. In the Democratic platform it states, "we will honor our sacred covenant with our women… We will work to ratify the Convention on the Elimination of All Forms of Discrimination Against Women. We will push for greater participation by women in the global workforce, which studies show can boost global GDP by 25 percent." The disciples of Jesus, Tabitha and Peter extended a hand to the poor and the widows honoring the sacred covenant to love one another.

A Canaanite woman confronts Jesus's perception of his purpose, "I was sent only to the lost sheep of Israel" (Matthew 15:21-28). In a human feeling of being overwhelmed, Jesus rebukes her as unworthy of his time. He compared her pleas as wasting his "bread of life," much like throwing scraps to the dogs under the table. The woman answers back promoting the life of the dog as well as herself. Jesus switches gears, acknowledges, listens, calls her a woman of faith, and heals her daughter.

Women in the Bible confront Jesus. Jesus is tested. The women are tested then blessed for their faith. Each year the Democratic platform is carefully crafted, tested, to bring it up to date on honoring the people. It pledges in its current form to switch gears, to acknowledge, to listen, and to reform racial, gender, Indigenous, religious, and differently-abled discrimination.

According to Ruth Bader Ginsberg, "You can disagree without being disagreeable."[7] In the Biblical stories of the women I have mentioned, the relationship with Jesus shows interaction. The women took risks to speak, disagree, love, trust, and believe. Jesus acknowledges these women, making them visible and heard by listening to their feelings and fulfilling God's promise to be with us.

[1] From John 2:4. All Bible references in this chapter come from the New International Version.
[2] Frankie Armstrong, performer, "Anti-Carol," by John Pole, *Out of Love, Hope and Suffering* (Bay Records, 1973).
[3] Dory Previn, performer, "Did Jesus have a Baby Sister," *Dory Previn* (Warner Records, 1974).
[4] Laura Bates, *Everyday Sexism* (Simon and Shuster, 2015), 21.
[5] All references to the Democratic platform taken from https://democrats.org/where-we-stand/party-platform/.
[6] Laurie Levin, *Call Me a Woman*, (One More Page Publishing, 2021), 44.
[7] Quoted in Laurie Levin, *Call Me a Woman*, (One More Page Publishing, 2021), 41.

George Lower graduated from Bucknell University in 1953, was drafted in the army, and sent to the Green Berets. After working for DuPont, he felt the call to be a Presbyterian pastor. His graduate education was two master's degrees, one from Pittsburgh Seminary and another in Religious Education from Hartford Seminary. His churches were in Anchorage, Alaska; Pittsburgh, Pennsylvania; Springville and Orem, Utah, and one international church in Kuala Lumpur, Malaysia. George's specialized ministries included two campus ministry positions, one at Edinboro State University in Pennsylvania, and ten years at Brigham Young University in Utah.

After Kuala Lumpur, George accompanied his wife Nancy to Mauritania (West Africa) where she was Medical Director for the Peace Corps. She had a fall and became a "quad." She was completely paralyzed for twenty years, but she remained in good spirits. Nancy and George have four daughters living in three different states. After Nancy's death, George and Linda Badoian had a "zoom" wedding and now live six winter months in Utah and six summer months at her island home in Islesboro, Maine.

Chapter Three

Jesus and the Democrats Care About Your Health and Healing

Rev. George H. Lower

The other day a group in the church were sitting around, and, before you realized it, we were talking about our health. Each person shared what was wrong with their health. What surgery they had recently had and what still needed to be done soon for the care of their body.

When we look at the Bible and the ministry of Jesus, we see that often he was asked to assist with health problems. People sought out Jesus and travelled many miles hoping Jesus could help them or a loved one with a health problem. Jesus healed the sick everywhere he went. When we look at every instance of Jesus healing in the Bible, what do they all have in common? In every instance of Jesus healing in the Bible, they all had this in common—FAITH. Jesus healed throughout the Bible, and we are going to examine where persons were healed who were not present.

Jesus Heals a Nobleman's Son at Capernaum in Galilee (John 4:43-54)

In verse 50 of this recording, it says that the nobleman "believed the word that Jesus spoke to him." Here was the faith in this instance. The nobleman believed Jesus when he said that his son would live. The faith of the person is what brings about healing. The nobleman had faith his son could be healed—and he was healed.

Jesus Heals a Centurion's Servant in Capernaum (Matthew 8:5-13, Luke 7:1-10)

The centurion was full of faith in this account, so much so that Jesus marveled and said he had not found such great faith in all of Israel. We see again a healing of a person not present—the faith of the centurion brought about the healing of his servant living miles away.

Faith is still the vital component when it comes to healing. Faith has to be present in a person who wants healing to take place. Jesus is present today as the Holy Spirit, and therefore the title of our book, *Jesus IS a Democrat*, shows that Jesus is alive today and cares about the healing of persons. Physical healing is a huge part of the ministry and is carried out by his followers.

The Healing Last Summer at the Second Baptist Church in Islesboro, Maine (August 2022)

Here is the story of the healing: It was a regular worship service with a time for members to share their concerns and prayers. A woman named Debbie stood up and shared how her husband had all these ailments and was also confined to his wheelchair. He could not walk. She sat down and others shared their concerns. After the service, I went up to her to talk about her husband and his ailments. I asked her if she believed in healing, which is done by God when a person has faith in healing. She said she had faith that God could heal her husband. I prayed with her for healing for her husband. We went back to the fellowship hour and spent time sharing with others. We went home for the week. We went back to the church the next week and Debbie was also present. We came to the area in the service for concerns. Debbie stood up and turned and looked directly at me and said, "When I went home, I found my husband OUT OF HIS WHEELCHAIR, and he was walking around!" She asked her husband what had happened to him. He said during her time at church he felt HE COULD WALK. So, he stood up and walked away from his wheelchair. Debbie found him walking when she got home from church. They rejoiced together and rejoiced with the congregation the next week. He is walking today and came to church for the first time in many months.

The issue here is that the FAITH of Debbie brought about the healing of her husband. Jesus is working today through the ministry of his followers. Jesus cares so much about seeing people well. His desire to see people on earth healed and whole is the same desire we find today in the Democratic Party in the United States.

Democrats Believe Health Care is a Right for All and Not a Privilege for the Few

Democrats have fought to achieve health care for a century. We are the party of Medicare, Medicaid, and the Affordable Care Act. Because of the Affordable Care Act, more than 100 million Americans with pre-existing conditions, from heart disease to asthma, are secure in the knowledge that insurance companies can no longer discriminate against them. Women can no longer be charged more than men just because of their gender. And more Americans are able to get health coverage than ever before.

Democrats will keep up the fight until all Americans can secure affordable, high-quality health care. Democrats are committed to protecting and advancing reproductive health, rights, and justice. We believe that every woman should be able to access high quality reproductive care services, including a legal and safe abortion. We believe that a person's health should always come first. Democrats will protect the rights of all people to make personal health care decisions. We are proud to be the party of the Affordable Care Act which prohibits discrimination in health care.

Conclusion on Health and Healing

Jesus cared about the health of people he met in his ministry. We are his followers, and we also care about the health of those we meet. The American way is to govern by electing persons and parties to carry out the wishes of the people. It appears to many that the Democrat Party seems to be able to "love our neighbor" and care about their health and well-being in an excellent way. Jesus has given us an example of loving and caring. We are happy to see our government leaders attempt in many ways to carry out this ministry as we care for the health of Americans.

Lois Aroian is a retired Presbyterian pastor, retired US diplomat, and published historian of the Middle East, North Africa, and Muslim world. Raised in Los Angeles, she has devoted her life to serving others. Lois's parents grew up in poor, immigrant families. They led Lois and her older sister Julie to lives of compassion, defending the oppressed, and giving to others. Lois's careers took her to a junior year abroad in Lebanon, research in Egypt, teaching in Nigeria, writing two Middle East histories, and US diplomatic service in Sudan, Morocco, Syria, Lebanon, Cyprus, Kenya (covering a fourteen-country region), Mauritania, Quebec City (Canada), and Botswana. She studied at the American University of Beirut and the American University in Cairo. She graduated from Occidental College (AB), The University of Michigan (AM, PhD), the National

War College of the National Defense University (MS), and Wesley Theological Seminary (MDiv with honors). Lois worked as a legislative aide for Representative Mervyn Dymally (D-California) in 1983-84 under the auspices of the Rockefeller Congressional Fellowship awarded by the American Historical Association. Ordained a minister in 2010, Lois has served churches in South Dakota and Michigan. She lives in East Jordan, Michigan, where she was president of the Rotary Club in 2021-22.

Chapter Four

Jesus's Preference for the Poor and the Democratic Party

Rev. Dr. Lois A. Aroian

On the face of it, Jesus's preference for the poor needs no introduction. However, because it is deeply-rooted in the scriptures of the Hebrew Bible, it merits some background. The most common term for the poor in the Greek Hebrew Bible and New Testament texts is *penixros*. It has many aspects. In an early reference in Exodus 22:25, it means "one without possessions," "very poor," and "quite needy."[1] The text says that "if you lend money to my people who are poor among you, don't be a creditor and charge them interest."[2] Dozens of Hebrew Bible references make the same point. Needy people should not be exploited. Compassion for the very poor is intrinsic to the Hebrew faith that Jesus inherited and studied. Greek lexicons amplify the various aspects of *penixros*. For example, in John 12:8, it means "poor, miserable, beggarly, impotent, poor in the world's goods, one dependent on others, of little value, one who cowers, crouches, or cringes."[3]

Another Greek word used in the New Testament for the poor is *ptochos,* from the verb *ptosso*. It means "to crouch." James Strong defines it as a pauper. This means "absolute or public mendicancy," though it can also be used in a "qualified or relative sense." In another context, it may mean "only straitened circumstances in private."[4]

Reflecting on each of these nuances, we come to understand the depth of what happens when individuals are poor. They lack power. This means they must depend on others. Perhaps, they have to beg others for help. Moreover, people view them as having little value. They cower and cringe in the face of a society that oppresses them. The word encompasses the idea of "roving about in wretchedness."

It goes farther. According to Thayer, this word *ptochos* connotes someone "destitute of wealth, influence, position, honour." In addition, it could mean "lowly, afflicted, destitute of the Christian virtues and eternal riches." Additionally, it means "destitute of wealth of learning and intellectual culture which the schools afford."[5]

In other words, in the New Testament, "poor" is far broader than material realities. It refers to social status, status within society, and even to status as a Christian. The word *ptochos* appears thirty-four times in the New Testament, in all four Gospels, Romans, 2 Corinthians, Galatians, James, and Revelation.[6]

From Matthew:

5:3: Blessed are the poor in spirit, for theirs is the kingdom of heaven.

6:2: Whenever you give to the poor, don't blow your trumpet as the hypocrites do in the synagogues and in the streets so that they may get praise from people. I assure you, that's the only reward they'll get. But when you give to the poor, don't let your left hand know what your right hand is doing so that you may give to the poor in secret. Your Father who sees what you do in secret will reward you.

11:5: The dead are raised up, and the poor have the gospel preached to them.

19:21: Jesus said, "If you want to be complete, go, sell what you own, and give the money to the poor. Then, you will get treasure in heaven."

From Mark:

10:21: He said, "You are lacking one thing. Go, sell what you own, and give the money to the poor. Then, you will have treasure in heaven."

From Luke:

4:18: Quoting Isaiah, "he has sent me to preach good news to the poor."

6:20: "Happy are you who are poor, because God's kingdom is yours."

14:13: "When you give a banquet, invite the poor, crippled, maimed, and blind."

18:22: When Jesus heard this, he said: "There's one more thing. Sell everything you have and distribute the money to the poor. Then, you will have treasure in heaven."

The gospel according to John is different. It speaks of love in the broadest sense, which includes keeping his commandments.

Jesus makes clear in these passages that he has a preference for the poor. He instructs us to sell what we have and give it to the poor. He tells us that when we host a dinner, we should invite the downtrodden, including the poor. He further says that we should not publicize our generosity. God will reward us.

In our review of Jesus, his life, and work, we can understand why, if Jesus were alive today, he would support what the Democratic Party stands for now.[7] In his life, Jesus appears to have avoided any connection with politics. He certainly would have had little in common with the Democratic Party of the nineteenth century.

The twentieth and twenty-first centuries have been different. Democrats led the movement in the 1930s to address the poverty caused by the Great Depression. These poverty-alleviation programs included:

- 1935: The Social Security Act (June 17, 1935). The bill included direct relief (cash, food stamps, etc.) and changes for unemployment insurance.
- 1940: Aid to Families with Dependent Children (AFDC).
- 1964: President Johnson's War on Poverty. Passage of the Economic Opportunity Act.
- 1996: The Personal Responsibility and Work Opportunity Reconciliation Act of 1996, passed under President Clinton, aimed to give people more opportunities to take charge of their lives.
- 2013: The Affordable Care Act went into effect with large increases in Medicaid and subsidized medical insurance premiums. Individuals could obtain health insurance, thereby helping them to avoid poverty-raising expenses.

In its most recent iteration, Democratic Party platforms promote principles of poverty-alleviation. These include social programs, communications and transportation, labor unions, equal opportunity, disability rights, racial equality, health and safety, and criminal justice reform.

The Democratic Party's 2020 Platform

Many principles of today's Democratic Party address poverty issues, both directly and indirectly. So many factors work together to disadvantage Americans mired in poverty. These are some of the areas in which the Democratic Party platform seeks to reduce poverty:

High Speed Internet: The Democratic Party recognizes that, in the twenty-first century, access to high-speed internet is essential for Americans to prosper. This is particularly true in the COVID era when many Americans are working at home. The party has made commitments to upgrade "rural, urban, and Tribal broadband infrastructure, offer low-income Americans subsidies for accessing high-speed internet, and invest in digital literacy training programs, so children and families and people with disabilities can fully participate in school, work, and life from their homes."

Racial Bias: Poverty cannot be alleviated without the elimination of racial bias in employment. The Democratic Party platform notes, "The wage gap between Black workers and white workers is higher today than it was 20 years ago. It takes a typical Black woman 19 months to earn what a typical white man earns in 12 months—and for typical Latinas and Native American women, it takes almost two years." It commits to increase funding for the Equal Employment Opportunity Commission and its authority to initiate directed investigations into civil rights violations. There is no reason that the United States should not be a country of equal opportunity for everyone.

Sick Days and Family Leave: Sick days and family leave make it possible for people to address illness and family issues without losing their paycheck. The Democratic Party is committed to ensuring that workers don't have to choose between caregiving and work.

Childcare: The Democratic Party recognizes that childcare expenses can substantially erode the financial well-being of families. It commits to investing in affordable childcare and universal preschool so that parents don't have to choose between working and staying home.

Rural Poverty: The Democratic Party is committed to raising the standard of living for America's farmworkers who "are essential to our economy, our communities, and our security."

Homeownership: The Democratic Party recognizes the historical discrimination that has excluded racial minorities from building wealth. It also notes that millions of Americans have no access to affordable housing, plunging many into homelessness. It supports expansion of affordable credit to help families of color, low-income families, and rural families.

Energy Upgrades: The Democratic Party commits to make "energy efficiency upgrades for millions of low-income households, affordable housing units, and public housing units in metropolitan and rural areas to save families money on their energy bills and provide safe and healthy homes." These are critical for lowering energy costs for the poorest Americans.

Homelessness: Homelessness is generally a sign of extreme poverty. The Democratic Party seeks to end homelessness in America by providing Section 8 housing support. Landlords will not be able to discriminate against them. Democrats believe in a housing-first approach for the poor, "because having a stable and safe place to live is essential to helping a person tackle any other challenges they may face, from mental illness to substance use disorders to post-traumatic stress disorder."

Redlining: The Democratic Party opposes use of public policy and private lending restrictions to close neighborhoods off to Black families and other People of Color and strip equity from their communities. The Trump Administration "made matters worse by gutting fair lending and fair housing protections for homeowners." Democrats seek to enforce legislation that bans housing discrimination.

> Democrats will give local elected officials tools and resources to combat gentrification, penalize predatory lending practices, and maintain homeownership, including exploring targeted rental relief when exorbitant rent increases force long-term residents from their communities and tackling persistent racial bias in appraisals that contributes to the racial wealth gap.

Reforming the Tax Code to Benefit Working Families: Democrats recognize that big corporations, aided by Republican politicians, have geared the tax code to benefit them instead of working Americans. Democrats commit to reforming the tax code to be more progressive and equitable and reduce barriers for working families to benefit from targeted tax breaks, including the Earned Income Tax Credit and the Child Tax Credit.

Access to Credit: To further poverty reduction, access to credit is critical. Democrats aim to create a public credit reporting agency to provide a non-discriminatory credit reporting alternative to the private agencies and will require its use by all federal lending programs, including home lending and student loans.

Bankruptcy: Democrats

commit to revisit and repeal sections of existing bankruptcy law that frequently lead to debtors losing their home as the result of medical debt, divorce, job loss, or just bad luck. We will also give bankruptcy judges the authority to 'cram down,' or modify, mortgages for primary residences during bankruptcy proceedings, so working families can benefit from the same debt relief tools currently available to those who own assets like vacation homes and yachts.

More Anti-Poverty Measures:

The Democratic Party

recognizes that the official poverty rate, as measured and communicated by the federal government, fails to capture critical needs like housing, education, health care, transportation, energy, and other necessities, and therefore understates the true share of Americans living in poverty. The Democratic Party will support the 10-20-30 funding approach, to direct at least 10 percent of federal funding to communities where 20 percent or more of the population has been living below the poverty line for 30 years or longer.

Minimum Wage: The Democratic Party seeks to raise the minimum wage to $15 an hour and guarantee equal pay for women, two measures that in combination will pull millions of families out of poverty.

Hunger: In the wealthiest country on earth, it is a moral abomination that any child could ever go to bed hungry. Democrats will increase funding for food assistance programs, including SNAP, WIC, and school meals. The Party commits to removing barriers that keep the formerly incarcerated from accessing food assistance, barriers that can keep them poor.

Legal Services: The Democratic Party recognizes that lack of legal services helps to keep people poor. It supports increasing investment in the Legal Services Corporation.

Democrats will promise substantially higher levels of support for programs and institutions that boost economic development in America's most impoverished communities, including by doubling funding for CDFIs, expanding the Community Development Block Grant, increasing the number of Rural Business Investment Companies, and expanding and making permanent the New Markets Tax Credit.

Bank Reform: Lack of access to banks keeps many Americans at risk of losing money due to "exorbitant fees or usurious interest rates." Democrats seek enhanced access to banking services for low- and middle-income families.

Social Security: The Democratic Party supports retirement security for everyone. This includes keeping Social Security, which Democrats created, strong. Democrats will reject every effort to cut, privatize, or weaken Social Security, including attempts to raise the retirement age, diminish benefits by cutting cost-of-living adjustments, or reduce earned benefits. We will ensure Social Security will be there forever.

Retirement Security: Democrats will protect Americans' retirement security, acting to protect public and private pensions to ensure workers keep the benefits they have earned, including through multiemployer plans. In addition, Democrats seek to ease the process of saving for retirement in general. They support amending federal bankruptcy laws to protect workers' earned pensions from being taken away by employers going through bankruptcy.

Reducing Health Care Costs: Americans have the highest medical costs in the developed world. The Affordable Care Act has reduced those costs for the poorest Americans. The lowest-income Americans, including more than four million adults who should be eligible for Medicaid but who live in states where Republican governors have refused to expand the program, will be automatically enrolled in the public option without premiums; they may opt out at any time. The party intends to enable millions of older workers to choose between their employer-provided plans, the public option, or enrolling in Medicare when they turn sixty, instead of having to wait until they are sixty-five. Democrats are categorically opposed to raising the Medicare retirement age.

Prescription Drugs: Democrats favor reducing the costs for prescription drugs. Medicare will be able to negotiate prescription drug prices for all public and private purchasers—for families and businesses, as well as older Americans—no matter where they get their coverage.

Criminal Justice: Democrats believe "our system has criminalized poverty, overpoliced and underserved Black and Latino communities, and cut public services." The system needs a total overhaul. We need to take actions to keep poor children out of the criminal justice system.

Cash Bail: Democrats support eliminating the use of cash bail and believe no one should be imprisoned merely for failing to pay fines or fees or have their driver's licenses revoked for unpaid tickets or simple violations.

Mobility for People of Color: The extreme gap in household wealth and income between People of Color—especially Black Americans, Latinos, Native Americans, and certain Asian American and Pacific Islander communities—and white families harms our working class and holds our country back. Democrats are committed to improving economic mobility for People of Color. We will fight to tackle intergenerational poverty and close the racial wealth gap. Democrats recognize that racial wealth gaps are rooted in long-standing discrimination and unjust policies. The party seeks to equalize established pathways for building wealth while exploring innovative approaches to closing racial wealth gaps, including policies that provide seed capital in order to access the economic security of asset ownership.

The Right to Organize and Bargain Collectively: This right benefits all workers, but especially for workers of color. Unions close pay gaps between white workers and People of Color. The union wage premium is high for all workers but remains especially substantial for People of Color, including Latino and Black workers. This is one reason why Black workers represent a higher share of the labor movement than the workforce as a whole.

Low Income Communities: The party plans investment in low-income communities, urban and rural areas, and communities of color by strengthening the Community Reinvestment Act, improving federal support and access to credit for women- and minority-owned small businesses, expanding and making permanent the New Markets Tax Credit, and doubling funding for CDFIs.

Safe Workplaces: Democrats aim to restore and build on the Obama-Biden Administration's Fair Pay and Safe Workplaces policy and use the purchasing power of the federal government to incentivize private companies to recruit and advance People of Color, women, people with disabilities, and veterans.

Keeping Americans with Disabilities Out of Poverty: Democrats will phase out the subminimum wage, expand competitive, integrated employment opportunities, and protect and strengthen economic security for people with disabilities. They plan to take a holistic approach to the Supplemental Security Income (SSI) and Social Security Disability Insurance (SSDI) programs that are essential for millions of Americans with disabilities by increasing SSI benefits, eliminating waiting periods for SSDI, and eliminating the "benefit cliff" for SSDI benefits. The platform promises to increase federal funding to expand accessible transportation and accessible, integrated, and affordable housing. Savings accounts, which provide people with disabilities a way to pay for disability-related expenses like housing, education, and transportation, will be set up. And Democrats will improve access to home- and community-based care for people with disabilities and older Americans, including by enforcing the Medicaid Home and Community-Based Settings Rule, ending the institutional bias within Medicaid, and expanding the home care workforce to end state waiting lists for long-term services and supports.

Tribal Lands: The platform promises measures to reduce poverty on tribal lands, especially by providing resources for economic development.

Climate Change: The platform notes that "Communities of color, low-income families, and Indigenous communities have long suffered disproportionate and cumulative harm from air pollution, water pollution, and toxic sites." It promises to

> invest in the education and training of underrepresented groups, including people of color, low-income Americans, women, veterans, people with disabilities, and unemployed energy workers for jobs in clean energy-related industries, especially union jobs that provide strong opportunities for economic advancement. Democrats will target relevant investments with the goal of delivering forty percent of the overall benefits to disadvantaged and frontline communities, including in clean energy and energy efficiency; clean transit and transportation; affordable and sustainable housing; remediation and reduction of legacy pollution; and critical clean water infrastructure.

Energy Costs: Democrats will lower families' energy bills by making energy-saving upgrades to up to two million low-income households and affordable and public housing units within five years, creating hundreds of thousands of jobs and promoting safe, healthy, and efficient homes. They will incentivize landlords to make energy efficiency and clean energy upgrades that will reduce their tenants' energy costs. Democrats will encourage states and cities to adopt energy-efficient building codes, address barriers to energy efficiency upgrades, incentivize the adoption of efficient electric and geothermal pump home heating solutions that can help reduce families' energy burden, and leverage the federal footprint to model net-zero and 100 percent clean energy building solutions.

Immigration: Democrats recognize that poverty is one of the major factors pushing individuals to immigrate to the United States.

Early Childhood Education: Democrats view education as a key means of poverty reduction. Early childhood education is crucial to giving children a head start. Democrats will direct resources to the poorest urban and rural communities as well as education for the disabled.

Supporting High-Quality K-12 Schools across America: Democrats are committed to closing the $23 billion funding gap between white and non-white districts, by tripling Title 1 funding, which benefits schools that serve low-income students. Democrats oppose private school vouchers and other policies that divert taxpayer-funded resources away from the public school system, including the program at issue in the recent Espinoza decision.

Making Higher Education Affordable and Accessible: Democrats believe that everyone should be able to earn a degree beyond high school, if they choose to, without money standing in the way. Democrats will make public colleges and universities tuition-free for students whose families earn less than $125,000— roughly eighty percent of the American people. We will double the maximum Pell Grant award for low-income students, and double federal support for TRIO programs that help first-generation college students, students with disabilities, veterans, and other underrepresented groups apply to and complete college. HBCUs, MSIs, and TCUs serve a disproportionate number of low-income students who might otherwise be unable to access a college degree, and yet these vital institutions are chronically under-resourced. Democrats will work to provide grants to HBCUs, MSIs, and TCUs to lower student costs, increase academic research capabilities, and ensure these essential institutions can continue to thrive in the future. Democrats support making community colleges and trade schools tuition-free for all students, including Dreamers.

Childcare, Textbooks, and Fees: Democrats will increase federal support for services like childcare on college campuses so more students are able to balance the demands of school and family and graduate with degrees. Democrats also support increased funding for wraparound services, including covering the cost of textbooks and fees for low-income students and establishing programs to address campus food insecurity so students can focus on what matters most: their studies.

Democrats will fight to create a federal funding program for higher education, modeled on Title I funding for K-12 schools, that would direct funds to public and nonprofit colleges and universities and minority-serving institutions based on the proportion of low-income students those schools enroll and graduate.

Providing Borrowers Relief from Crushing Student Debt: Student debt has impoverished millions of Americans. Democrats will work to authorize up to $10,000 in student debt relief per borrower to help families weather this crisis. Beyond that immediate relief, Democrats will also take steps to ease the burden of high monthly student loan payments through legislative and administration relief processes, including creating a simplified repayment process. Democrats will work to pause monthly billing and stop interest from accruing on federal student loans for people earning less than $25,000 and cap payments at no more than five percent of discretionary income for those earning more than $25,000. After twenty years, remaining federal student loan debt should be automatically forgiven without tax liability. For those earning less than $125,000, we support forgiving all undergraduate tuition-related federal student debt from two- and four-year public colleges and universities, and we will also apply this benefit to individuals holding federal student loans for tuition from private HBCUs and MSIs.

Democrats support modernizing and improving the Public Service Loan Forgiveness program, including making the enrollment process automatic for people who work in schools, government agencies, and non-profit organizations. Not only will these measures make it easier for Americans to buy a home or start a small business, but student debt forgiveness is key to helping address the racial wealth gap, as students of color are more likely to have to borrow to finance higher education. Democrats will also empower the CFPB to take action against exploitative lenders and will work with Congress to allow student debt to be discharged during bankruptcy.

Wage Gap: The extreme gap in household wealth and income between People of Color—especially Black Americans, Latinos, Native Americans, and certain Asian American and Pacific Islander communities—and white families is hurting our working class and holding our country back. Democrats are committed to improving economic mobility for People of Color. We will fight to tackle intergenerational poverty and close the racial wealth gap. Democrats recognize that racial wealth gaps are rooted in long-standing discrimination and unjust policies. We will equalize established pathways for building wealth while exploring innovative approaches to closing racial wealth gaps, including policies that provide seed capital in order to access the economic security of asset ownership.

Justice and Fairness for Immigrants: Democrats know that when employers feel free to abuse and bully immigrant workers, all workers suffer. That's why we will hold employers accountable, promote workers' rights, and prioritize the enforcement of labor and employment laws across the economy, including discrimination and sexual harassment protections, wage and hour laws, and health and safety rules. We will prevent employers from taking advantage of immigrant workers by establishing an affirmative process to request deferred action for workers who report labor violations and by supporting the Domestic Workers' Bill of Rights and the Protect Our Workers from Exploitation and Retaliation (POWER) Act.

President Biden's Priorities: President Biden proposed a "Build Back Better Framework" (BBB) to grow the US economy from the bottom up.[8] The BBB advocated "the most transformative investment in children and care-giving in generations." It sought to save Americans more than half their current spending on childcare. Universal and free preschool for all three- and four-year-olds was part of the plan. It would provide tax cuts for the poorest Americans with children. President Biden sought a huge expansion in health care, including reductions in the cost of prescription drugs. The BBB also included bringing down the cost of housing and providing nutrition security to millions of children.

The Platform: A Miracle When a Bill Becomes a Law

These platform goals make clear that the Democratic Party is on the side of the poor, as Jesus was. In reality, however, platforms do not necessarily translate into law, especially in the midst of divisive politics. Of the hundreds of bills proposed by members of the 117th Congress (2021-22), only 362 actually passed.[9] A large tranche of these successful bills, forty-two in all, renamed various buildings, especially US Post Office buildings, in the legislators' home states or towns. The Congress also passed a large number of laws that addressed issues pertaining to veterans.

The 117th Congress passed omnibus bills proposed by Democrats that addressed poverty issues. These incorporated provisions of some of those smaller bills and fulfilled many of the Democratic Party's platform priorities. These were:

HR 1319: The American Rescue Plan of 2021 (PL No: 117-2), 3/11/21:
    Some of its provisions relating to poverty were:
    Direct stimulus payments
    Moratoriums on evictions and foreclosures
    Child tax credits
    Child nutrition
    Home energy cost mitigation
    Tax credits for health plans for low and middle-income taxpayers
    Extensive aid to farmers.
    $3 billion for disabled communities' transportation
    Extension of unemployment benefits
    Childcare and block grants
    Assistance to both public and non-public schools, especially high-poverty schools

Homelessness

Emergency rural development grants

Housing vouchers

HR 3684: Infrastructure Investment and Jobs Act (PL No: 117-58), 11/15/21:

This measure focused on "left behind" communities, impoverished by lack of transportation, limited access to clean drinking water, lack of high-speed internet, and pollution. With Biden's Build Back Better Framework, it expects to add 1.5 million jobs per year on average for the next ten years.

HR 5376: Inflation Reduction Act of 2022 (PL No: 117-169), 8/16/2022:

Expanded Medicare for impaired older Americans.

Lowered prescription drug prices.

Provided subsidies for the Affordable Care Act.

Several consolidated appropriations acts and emergency supplementals (LAW 117-103, 117-328, 117-70) incorporated poverty reduction measures. Smaller laws passed to alleviate poverty included the Keep Kids Fed Act (LAW 117-158 of 6/25/2022).

Despite Democratic control of both houses, the 117th Congress could not pass a legislative package that contained all of the Democrats' platform promises. The problems ensued from Republican refusal to support the Democratic agenda and divisions within the Democratic Party itself.

The progressive wing of the Democratic Party insisted on inclusion of the broad range of social programs within Biden's Build Back Better program while two Senators, Senator Kyrsten Sinema of Arizona and Senator Joe Manchin of West Virginia, advocated lower-cost legislation that omitted most of these social programs. Negotiations over provisions dragged on for months. In the end, many social programs were cut from these key bills. Prospects for their being revived by the 118th Congress are poor due to the Republican Party's new majority in the House of Representatives.

We Christians recognize that Jesus himself sought to disentangle himself from the overtly political aspirations of many of his followers. He famously said to a group of Pharisees who sought to entrap him by asking if the Hebrews should pay taxes (as quoted in Mark 12:17), "Give to Caesar what belongs to Caesar and to God what belongs to God." For this reason, it is very difficult to conclude that Jesus would be a card-carrying Democrat in this day and age. On the other hand, certainly Jesus, with his over-riding concern for the poor, is a Democrat in spirit.

---

[1] Timothy Friburg, Barbara Friburg, and Neva F. Miller, *Analytical Greek Lexicon* (Trafford Publishing, 2005); Johannes Louw and Eugene Nida, *Greek-English Lexicon of the New Testament* (United Bible Societies, 1988); Henry Liddell, Robert Scott, Henry Stuart Jones, and Roderick McKenzie, eds., *Greek Lexicon,* 9th edition, (Clarendon Press, 1996); Joseph Thayer, *Thayer's Greek-English Lexicon of the New Testament,* (Hendrickson's Academic, 1995); Felix Wilbur Gingrich, *Greek New Testament Lexicon* (Chicago University Press, 1965); R. Laird Harris and Gleason Archer, Jr., *Theological Wordbook of the Old Testament* (Chicago: Moody Press, 1980); James Strong, John Kohlenberger, III, and James Swanson, *The Strongest Strong's Exhaustive Concordance of the Bible* (Zondervan, 2001). Cited using Bibleworks 9 software.

[2] The English Bible texts are drawn from the *Common English Bible.*

[3] Idem; J. H. Moulton and G. Milligan, *Vocabulary of the Greek New Testament*, (Baker Academic, 1995).

[4] Thayer Timothy Friburg, Barbara Friburg, and Neva F. Miller, *Analytical Greek Lexicon* (Trafford Publishing, 2005); Johannes Louw and Eugene Nida, *Greek-English Lexicon of the New Testament* (United Bible Societies, 1988); Henry Liddell, Robert Scott, Henry Stuart Jones, and Roderick McKenzie, eds., *Greek Lexicon,* 9th edition, (Clarendon Press, 1996); Joseph Thayer, *Thayer's Greek-English Lexicon of the New Testament,* (Hendrickson's Academic, 1995).

[5] Joseph Thayer, *Thayer's Greek-English Lexicon of the New Testament,* (Hendrickson's Academic, 1995).

[6] Use of *Bibleworks 9* facilitated discovery of these lexicons and the word counts.

[7] Found on the website Democrats.org/where-we-stand/party-platform/. Much of the text and commentary that follows is a direct quotation from the platform.

[8] "The Build Back Better Framework: President Biden's Plan to Rebuild the Middle Class," The White House (website), www.whitehouse.gov/build-back-better.

[9] All of the information about legislation in this section comes from the www.congress.gov.

Melody Oliphant serves as a Ruling Elder in her church community and is currently studying in the Certificate in Ministry program. She loves being a mom and a grandma. Melody lives with her husband and son along with her cats, dog, fish, guinea pigs, and chickens.

Chapter Five

Immigration: Welcoming the Stranger

Melody Oliphant

Jesus would be a Democrat. The two parties are not the same.

In writing this chapter, I turned to the Democratic National Committee platform regarding immigration. What I found was an article titled, "Creating a 21st Century Immigration System."[1] What I discovered in reading through it was that there are a lot of reforms that are needed, mostly because of issues brought about by the Trump Administration. To understand where we are heading, we need to remember where we just came from, so here is a brief recap.

From the time that Donald Trump was president, chaos, racism, Islamophobia, and hatred was the law of the land under the names of "zero-tolerance" policy, travel bans from Muslim countries, and ICE raids. The zero-tolerance policy in 2018 created horrific changes to the immigration policy. At the border, children and parents were ripped from one another's arms and sent off separately to different detention facilities; they were given emergency blankets (essentially foil sheets) to keep warm in storehouses and thin sleeping mats; children changed babies' diapers; and everything was done in secret and secure buildings where admittance wasn't given.[2]

A ninety-day ban on travel from Muslim countries affected hundreds of refugees, many of whom were on flights to the United States when the ban went into effect. Many attorneys went to the airports late at night to see to the refugees' safety since they were not allowed into the country.[3]

Trump, in talking about Haiti and African nations, wondered aloud at one point as to why we allow immigrants from "shithole nations" to come to America—why not from Norway? "The U.N. human rights office said the comments, if confirmed, were 'shocking and shameful' and 'racist.'"[4]

During the Trump Era (2017-2021), story after story about raids from ICE were as commonplace as they were horrific. One such story was about a ten-year-old girl with cerebral palsy who was immediately taken to a detention center after having gallbladder surgery, even though she had relatives who were US citizens that she could have been released to.[5] There are many news articles showing the chaos and terror that were commonplace for immigrants during the Trump years.

Turning back to the here and now, the Democrats' stance on immigration, and the article "Creating a 21st Century Immigration System," found on www.democrats.org, I feel heartened that our country can turn things around and go in a direction that my Christian values tell me we should. I appreciate their honesty in the article when they state, "The truth is that our immigration system was broken long before President Trump came into office, and his departure alone won't fix it."

The article goes on to state that

> Immigrants are essential to our society and our economy. Immigrants are part of our families. They enrich our culture. They

grow our food, care for our loved ones, serve in our armed forces, and provide critical health care services. Immigrants make America stronger. Not only do immigrants support us—immigrants are us. Our families and our communities, our congregations and our schools, our businesses large and small have been built and sustained through the inclusion of immigrants. That's why Democrats commit to building a 21st century immigration system that reflects our values, repairs past harms, heals our communities, rebuilds our economy, and renews our global leadership.

We will immediately terminate the Trump Administration's discriminatory travel and immigration bans that disproportionately impact Muslims, Arab, and African people, and invite those whose visas have been denied under these xenophobic and un-American policies to re-apply to come to the United States. We will support legislation to ensure that no president can enact discriminatory bans ever again.

The ideals above taken from the article "Creating a 21st Century Immigration System" tell me that Democrats believe in dismantling racism. Racism plays a very big role in unfair treatment for immigrants—especially immigrants who are People of Color; racism is the underlying reason behind Trump's "shithole country" comment.

The ideals from the Democratic Party's platform are the same as those that I read in the Bible. In Galatians 3:26-28, we read that "for in Christ Jesus you are all children of God through faith…There is no longer Jew or Greek; there is no longer slave or free; there is no longer male and female, for all of you are one in Christ Jesus." Matthew 25:35-36 tells us that Jesus wants us to feed the hungry, give water to the thirsty, welcome the stranger, clothe the naked, care for the sick, visit the prisoner and that these are the things that we will be judged for.

Isn't that what it sounds like when the Democrats want to guarantee the safety and dignity of those in detention centers, giving those with special vulnerabilities (the elderly, pregnant or nursing, those with serious physical or mental illness, those with disabilities, those who are gay, lesbian, transgender, intersex, and gender non-conforming) alternatives to traditional detention centers?[6]

The values of keeping families intact as a family unit as often as possible, prohibiting raids in areas where children and caretakers can easily get separated, providing competent interpreters who speak the migrants' language and dialects inside of detention centers, and holding workers accountable for inappropriate, unlawful, or inhumane treatment of detained migrants is the goal of the Democratic Party.

It sounds very similar to the spirit of Jesus's message—The Greatest Commandment:

> Hearing that Jesus had silenced the Sadducees, the Pharisees got together. One of them, an expert in the law, tested him with this question: 'Teacher, which is the greatest commandment in the Law?' Jesus replied: 'Love the Lord your God with all your heart and with all your soul and with all your mind.' This is the first and greatest commandment. And the second is like it: 'Love your neighbor as yourself.' All the Law and the Prophets hang on these two commandments (Matthew 22:34-40).

Jesus was a Jew. He read from the Hebrew scriptures. He knew them, and he taught them. In that vein, let's not forget what the Hebrew scriptures have to say about "strangers" in their land:

> The alien who resides with you shall be to you as the native-born among you; you shall love the alien as yourself, for you were aliens in the land of Egypt: I am the Lord your God (Leviticus 19:34).

> When you reap your harvest in your field and forget a sheaf in the field, you shall not go back to get it; it shall be left for the alien, the orphan, and the widow, so that the Lord your God may bless you in all your undertakings. When you beat your olive trees, do not strip what is left; it shall be for the alien, the orphan, and the widow. When you gather the grapes of your vineyard, do not glean what is left; it shall be for the alien, the orphan, and the widow. Remember that you were a slave in the land of Egypt; therefore I am commanding you to do this (Deuteronomy 24:19–22).

> Do not neglect to show hospitality to strangers, for by doing that some have entertained angels without knowing it (Hebrews 13:2).

As Christians, we believe in a God of love, a God who chose to come down and live among us in the meagerest of circumstance, a God who taught us to love each other as we love ourselves, a God who forgives us when we miss the mark and sin, but who encourages us to be the best we can be. With that love, it is our job to go forward and live into the message that Jesus himself taught us to pray:

> Our Father, Who art in heaven,
> Hallowed be Thy Name.
> Thy Kingdom come.
> Thy Will be done,
> on earth as it is in Heaven.
>
> Give us this day our daily bread.
> And forgive us our trespasses,
> as we forgive those who trespass against us.

And lead us not into temptation,
but deliver us from evil.
Amen.

Jesus taught us how to live. He taught us how to treat each other. He modeled it for us. It is up to us to try to live into the Christian theme of doing God's will, which according to the Lord's Prayer is to help him bring his kingdom to the earth. The way to do that was told in simple language to the Pharisee: "'Love the Lord your God with all your heart and with all your soul and with all your mind.' This is the first and greatest commandment. And the second is like it: 'Love your neighbor as yourself.' All the Law and the Prophets hang on these two commandments."

In closing, I'd like to remind you who your neighbor is according to a story Jesus told of the Good Samaritan found in the Gospel of Luke 10:25-37:

> An expert in the law stood up to test Jesus. "Teacher," he said, "what must I do to inherit eternal life?" He said to him, "What is written in the law? What do you read there?" He answered, "You shall love the Lord your God with all your heart and with all your soul and with all your strength and with all your mind and your neighbor as yourself." And he said to him, "You have given the right answer; do this, and you will live."
>
> But wanting to vindicate himself, he asked Jesus, "And who is my neighbor?" Jesus replied, "A man was going down from Jerusalem to Jericho and fell into the hands of robbers, who stripped him, beat him, and took off, leaving him half dead. Now by chance a priest was going down that road, and when he saw him, he passed by on the other side. So likewise a Levite, when he came to the place and saw him, passed by on the other side.
>
> But a Samaritan while traveling came upon him, and when he saw him, he was moved with compassion. He went to him and bandaged his wounds, treating them with oil and wine. Then he

put him on his own animal, brought him to an inn, and took care of him. The next day he took out two denarii, gave them to the innkeeper, and said, 'Take care of him, and when I come back, I will repay you whatever more you spend.' Which of these three, do you think, was a neighbor to the man who fell into the hands of the robbers?" He said, "The one who showed him mercy."

Jesus said to him, "Go and do likewise."

---

[1] Democratic Party, "Creating a 21st Century Immigration System," Where We Stand, https://democrats.org/where-we-stand/party-platform/creating-a-21st-century-immigration-system/.

[2] Maegan Vazquez, "Dem Senator Accuses Trump Admin of 'Cruel' Effort Against Immigrant Children," (www.cnn.com, Mon June 4, 2018).

[3] Jonah Engel Bromwich, "Lawyers Mobilize at Nation's Airports After Trump's Order," *New York Times*, (www.nytimes.com, Jan. 29, 2017).

[4] Ali Vitali, Kasie Hunt, and Frank Thorp V, "Trump Referred to Haiti and African Nations as 'Shithole' Countries," *NBC News,* (www.nbsnews.com, Jan. 11, 2018).

[5] Beatriz Alvarado, "Child with Cerebral Palsy Facing Immigration Detention after Surgery," *USA Today*, (www.usatoday.com, Oct 25, 2017).

[6] Democratic Party, "Creating a 21st Century Immigration System," Where We Stand, https://democrats.org/where-we-stand/party-platform/creating-a-21st-century-immigration-system/.

Made in the USA
Columbia, SC
22 June 2023